GLUTEN AND G COOKING IN ~~PERFECT~~ HARMONY

The One Recipe Solution to Accommodate Everyone

Lucie Cote Contente

Table of Contents

RECIPES

Why This Book?

After years of seeing nutritionists, searching the web, speaking to other gluten free people and even just going out to restaurants, I realized there wasn't a lot of support for people newly diagnosed as gluten free so I created my blog-glutenfree-notbychoice.com. It is full of information and recipes. I even had business size cards made up because it seemed like everywhere I went someone would be gluten free or they knew someone who was so I would give them a card. Through my blog I was able to see that people from all around the world went on it. I even created a Facebook page, glutenfree-notbychoice to try and reach more and more people but I still felt I wasn't reaching enough people. In order to spread the word that gluten free can be healthy and tasty, I decided to write this book.

We all lead busy lives. What makes this book different from other gluten free books is that the recipes are made for food diverse families-people with and without gluten free issues and creating one recipe for the whole family with one little tweak-a "root recipe". Let me explain. The main part of the recipe is like a tree trunk or the part everyone can eat. Then, imagine the roots of the tree, where you separate the main mixture and add the gluten free/non gluten free ingredient to complete the recipe. These recipes were created for people who don't want to cook two meals in a household where not everyone is gluten free. The best part is that the gluten free person gets to eat exactly what the non gluten free person eats.

There are so many times when you leave your house as a gluten free person that you don't feel "normal" when going to various places such as carnivals, festivals, restaurants and even house parties. Why not feel normal at home? I like to cook with basic ingredients that are already in your kitchen. This was the inspiration for my book.

The Beginning of My Journey

Hello, my name is Lucie and I have to eat gluten free. Back in July of 2009 I started having severe pain in my stomach and it felt like someone was punching me in the gut. After consulting with a Gastroenterologist (GI), the decision was made to remove my gall bladder. After four weeks of healing, my stomach was bloated and the pain had not subsided. The doctor then prescribed omeprazole for my heartburn, but this only proved to be an ineffective band-aid as my stomach remained bloated and I was still in a lot of pain. Since I didn't know what to eat to stop the pain, I decided to see a nutritionist.

The first nutritionist I saw recommended that I try omitting gluten from my diet. It's very difficult to accept the thought of not being able to eat gluten when most of your life you have. For two years I stayed away from bread and pasta as I thought those were the only foods that contained gluten. I felt better, but I still had stomach aches. I became my own Sherlock Holmes, and this investigation led to the realization that I had to omit a lot more from my diet than just bread and pasta. I learned that gluten can take 24-48 hours to process through your system so you really have to pay close attention to what you eat. I then started keeping a food diary to track what I ate on a daily basis. I was amazed at the number of products that actually had gluten in them. I didn't get much information as to what foods I could eat to lead a productive life and to feel "normal", so I started researching the internet about the foods I ate and whether they contained any gluten. Realizing my limited diet options, I then continued my search to find foods without gluten in them to incorporate in my daily food life.

Between 2009-2014, I learned a lot about what foods had gluten in them. It was a trial and error period with food resulting in some good and bad days. During this time I saw a few more nutritionists and one even told me to only eat salads! Only eat salads for the next 30 years?! I thought my life was over (ok, a bit dramatic but it was overwhelming). Ok, who doesn't like to eat a salad occasionally? I do, but not every day! I tried eating only salads for four straight days but that was too much roughage for my stomach!

There were lots of food experimentations. I tried basic foods... meats, vegetables, fruit, rice and potatoes, but sometimes trying to eat gluten free is not as easy as it sounds. A lifetime of eating just gluten free is a really long time! At this point in my journey even though I had seen multiple nutritionists and continued doing gluten free research on the internet, I thought I had been eating 100% gluten free but my stomach was still bothering me.

In 2014 I started a new job. One day my supervisor and I were talking about diets. She mentioned she loved the South Beach diet so I checked it out and found there was a gluten free version. I was doing great, but at the end of the first week I had what I thought was a gluten "episode" although I hadn't had gluten that I was aware of. I had no idea what happened so I tried the diet a second week and again I was sick at the end of the week. That was it! I finally made an appointment with a GI specialist and she sent me for three tests: SIBO (small intestinal bacteria overgrowth), genetic testing for celiac disease (I couldn't have the regular blood test because I had been off gluten for years) and lactose intolerance test. A few weeks later I met with the same specialist and she told me I had all three! SIBO was easily fixed with medication. I had a very high propensity of celiac disease (which meant I had it now or will in the near future) and now I couldn't have dairy? I was in shock! In hindsight it probably will sound silly to some, but I looked at the specialist and asked "what CAN I eat?"

I realized then that my life with food was never going to be the same again. I wished my younger self knew that this was going to be my future, I would have never taken foods with gluten for granted. The doctor was surprised too. She said you will need to eat a paleo diet. I didn't even know what that was! I walked out of that office visit happy that I knew what was wrong but so sad to know I would be "different" when it came to food for the rest of my life. And then my food research started again.

The reason I am sharing this information with you is because I have been able to help other people with similar symptoms and offer them hope. They have gone to their specialist and have had these same tests done and they feel better now. I was really lucky my specialist knew to test me for all of these things and to help me get a much better quality of life.

From that day on I stopped eating any dairy products (of course I had to look online to see which foods contained dairy because I was not taking any chances. I admit that psychologically it was hard for me to make all these food changes. My family was able to have gluten and dairy. The meals became a little boring at first. Meat, rice, potato and a vegetable-every day! I found some gluten free recipes on line but even though the pictures looked appetizing, the food didn't taste great. Most of the time the recipes had ingredients I had never even heard of or just didn't have in my kitchen. I started taking my original recipes and making them gluten free. My family didn't even notice the changes. I have tried so many variations of foods-some good, some not so good. It became a passion of mine. I believed then and still believe now that gluten free is not an end to great tasting food. After one year, I started reincorporating dairy products to see if I could tolerate any. I figured out I could have some in moderation. I realized that as a result of being off of dairy products, I didn't have heartburn anymore so I was able to stop taking omeprazole. I also noticed my face didn't break out anymore.

Knowledge Is Power

I feel like my survival skills kicked in at some point. I started reading anything I could about gluten; where it came from, why my parent's generation didn't have a problem, how is it affecting my body, why doesn't everyone have a problem and how can I make my food world better. I found many articles that were very helpful in my search for understanding what gluten is and how to eat gluten free.

Here is my summary of some of the information I found on my journey:

Wheat was not part of our diet thousands of years ago, we mostly ate meat, fruit and vegetables but through the centuries and the agricultural revolution our diets changed and our nutrients depleted. The breads of today are not like your grandmother made in the early 1900's. Do you remember how she let the dough rise overnight? The longer the dough rose, the more the fermentation process broke down the gluten, leaving small traces of gluten, if any. Today's instant yeast leaves no time for the fermentation process. With almost three million people having celiac disease, most people aren't aware they have it. So, what I've learned is keep it simple and eat more like what your ancestors would have eaten back in the 1800's.

Through my own experience and research people with celiac disease tend to have vitamin deficiency. After a few years I started noticing low energy, hair falling out and feeling anxious. I called my primary care doctor and she had me do blood tests. I also checked the internet to see what the reasons could be. I read that most people with celiac disease will be vitamin B deficient. My tests came back with low vitamin D. I started taking multivitamins and vitamin D. Please make sure to talk to your doctor about vitamin deficiency and to get them checked. If you can, take a gluten free multivitamin.

Unfortunately, when you first find out you have a gluten allergy and change your diet, you might gain weight. The reasons: when you ate gluten, you were sick and probably had diarrhea or vomited so you were not able to absorb the nutrients. Now that you feel better and are eating gluten free food you are eating more than when you were sick. Most prepackaged processed gluten free food are high in calories, fat, sugar and low in nutrients.

There were days I just didn't feel like cooking so I would get take-out but that wasn't always a good option, especially with my food allergies. The easy days of fast foods were gone! I started checking out local restaurant menus online and I would call some to see if they offered gluten free food. Sounds easy right? Nope, there are some restaurants where they claimed to serve me gluten free food but I would still somehow get sick. Some restaurants, waiters, chefs don't realize how important it is to not cross contaminate and to make sure everything you get is truly gluten free. Also, I checked to see if there were local gluten free or gluten free vegan bakeries around.

From the day you are diagnosed with a food allergy your road may seem long, but when you find a great restaurant or bakery that offers gluten free food or after cooking my gluten free recipes, the road will not seem so awful.

We gluten free people need to help each other. You can get empathy from loved ones and friends, but until they are on this journey they just can't understand how hard this can be at times.

Grocery Shopping

When I first found out about my food allergies and knew I had to go to the grocery store to find food I could eat, I was overwhelmed! I had no idea what I could eat. I started reading every label looking for wheat because that is all I thought gluten was. Grocery shopping took forever! I eventually found out that I should avoid malt, which then made the shopping process longer. I was thankful my children were not small anymore because I was on a mission, I had to focus at the grocery store and be diligent. I eventually found the ShopWell App. There might be other apps that do the same thing, but I use this one. The app is free and it made a big difference in my shopping experience. After you download the app, you fill out what foods you are trying to avoid and for what reason-like food allergies or if your goal is to lose weight. Once you establish what foods or ingredients you are trying to avoid, this app scans the product bar code and it alerts you to anything that you requested to avoid. Years later I still use this on new items. It's quick and easy and I haven't seen any discrepancies. Grocery shopping is necessary, but it shouldn't have to be filled with anxiety. Please remember if you have a gluten allergy to always use gluten free ingredients when cooking my recipes.

Getting Ready

Start with the foods you do not have to add anything to but that still taste great! I'm talking about fruits, vegetables, milk, cheese, nuts, rice, potatoes and meats, "clean eating" foods with one ingredient. Depending on where you live and your local weather, you can plant a garden to get the freshest vegetables, fruits and herbs. Local grocery stores have a great variety of all these products. There is a risk of eating gluten if you start adding products to these foods. Cold fruity drinks during the summer are great but a lot of alcohols and drink mixes have gluten in them. Packaged seasonings for meats have gluten in them. Soy sauce and gravy have gluten in them. Packages of rice with packages of seasonings have gluten in them. I hope this is starting to make sense. So many foods and drinks have gluten in them that I never even knew I was eating or drinking.

When you start eating gluten free most people think that people around you also have to eat gluten free. Even when you bring food to a party or a get together you should bring something you can eat. No one thinks about gluten more than people like us who deal with gluten intolerance every day. People just don't understand how much food we cannot eat. Just so you know I am the only one in this family with food allergies. My husband and four children are able to eat anything. So when I cook, I try to make it so they don't realize they are missing gluten. Don't know what to make for your next meal or dessert? In this book are recipes for breakfast, lunch, dinner and dessert that my family loves to eat.

Please note I am not a nutritionist, but I have spent years learning from them throughout my journey. Most of these recipes have either been passed down to me by family or friends or I took one of my own existing recipes and made them gluten free. I believe you will enjoy these recipes, my family and friends do. I am also not a professional chef, I just want to make your gluten free life better.

Always Be Prepared

I admit it, being gluten free makes me feel "different" than other people who don't have food restrictions. Add another food allergy like dairy intolerance and sometimes it's overwhelming.

Living in New England there are lots of outdoor festivals during the warmer May-October months. At simple things like a carnival, Octoberfest, baseball or football games to name a few, what do you eat? It's times like these that are stressful if you don't plan ahead. It's very rare that these events would have non contaminated gluten free food, so always bring something you can eat with you.

I always carry something that I can eat in my pocketbook in case I am out doing errands or visiting friends and family and I get hungry. It's very comforting to know you don't have to do without. Simple things like raisins, nuts, sunflower seeds, gluten free granola bars just to name a few. Remembering your snack will make you a happier person

When I want to try a new restaurant I always go on their website or call them and ask if they have a gluten free menu. It alleviates a lot of stress, especially if you are going out with friends. It helps to plan ahead and enjoy your time out.

All the articles in this book were helpful to me on my gluten free journey. After reading the articles and cooking the recipes, you will understand your gluten free life and you will be excited about eating delicious foods again!

GF & AF expo

There is a Gluten & Allergen Free expo that travels around the United States. I found out about it a couple of years ago and have gone ever since. This is one place you go and feel that everything you eat is safe. You feel normal! This Expo is amazing! Do NOT go there unless you have an empty stomach because you eat a lot of food! I also walked out with three big bags of gluten free treats to try. If you want to go to a local expo, check to see where the next one is at **www.gfafexpo.com**. It allows you to try a lot of new foods that you can incorporate into your daily diet. Most of the vendors have the product there for you to buy also. Everyone is there because they either have a food allergy or someone they know does. You meet a lot of nice people. I recommend this expo to everyone.

The following information is from Dr. Osborne—The Gluten Free Warrior, he says "please don't be stingy and share the knowledge by passing this post along"

43 Gluten Facts That Doctors Should Get, but Usually Don't

1. Everyone with celiac disease is gluten sensitive, but not everyone with gluten sensitivity will develop celiac disease
2. There are over 200 medical conditions that gluten can either cause, contribute to, or make worse.
3. Gluten can cause autoimmune disease
4. Gluten can cause leaky gut
5. Gluten is a common cause of unexplained iron deficiency anemia
6. Gluten is a common cause of vitamin B12 deficiency
7. There is a form of gluten in corn that can cause inflammatory damage
8. There is no such thing as a gluten free oat
9. Excessive gluten consumption can cause both excessive weight gain or loss
10. Lab tests for celiac disease aren't specific and have a tendency to deliver false negatives
11. Villous atrophy can also be caused by corn, soy, dairy, and parasite infections.
12. Eating processed "gluten free' food products is a bad idea
13. Some medications have been shown to mimic gluten sensitivity
14. Gluten can cause asthma symptoms
15. Vitamin C can help heal inflammatory damage caused by gluten.
16. Gluten can cause dizziness and loss of balance (Ataxia)
17. Gluten can cause seizures

18. Gluten is a migraine headache trigger

19. Gluten can contribute to testosterone problems in men.

20. Gluten can cause thyroid disease

21. Gluten can cause nerve pain and neuropathy

22. Gluten can cause 4 types of skin disease

23. Gluten can cause damage in doses as low as 20 ppm (1 breadcrumb)

24. Gluten sensitivity is completely different from a wheat allergy

25. Gluten can cause liver damage

26. Gluten can cause your gallbladder to malfunction

27. Casein, a protein in dairy, can mimic gluten

28. There are thousands of different kinds of gluten proteins found in grains

29. Sometimes gluten gets blamed for health problems that are caused by exposure to pesticides

30. Sometimes gluten gets blamed for health problems caused by other proteins found in grain.

31. Children with learning disorders often respond well to a gluten free diet

32. Processed food can be cross contaminated with gluten up to 41% of the time.

33. As many as 92% of the people following a gluten free diet continue to have health problems because of cross contamination, processed food, and consumption of corn, rice, sorghum and other grains.

34. Gluten can be found in orthodontic materials

35. It can take 3 years to fully recover from gluten induced disease.

36. Gluten free on the label doesn't make the food healthy.

37. The best way to lab test for gluten sensitivity issues is measuring DNA

38. Most doctors are as in the dark about gluten as the average person because the focus in medical school is nutrition deprived

39. Gluten can cause arthritis and joint pain

40. Gluten can cause IBS

41. The gluten free diet is not dangerous to follow if you don't have gluten sensitivity
42. Gluten in cosmetics and skin products can cause health problems
43. You can take a quick and easy quiz to help you determine whether going gluten free is a good idea for you

Medications, Alcohol, Candy

When I first started having stomach issues, I tried some over the counter medications and things got worse. It took a while before I looked them up online and found out those medications had gluten in them, I didn't even consider that was an option. So I looked up all my medications in my house to make sure they were gluten free. Make sure you check all your medications to stay safe.

I never realized that some alcohols also contain gluten. But the good news is there are a lot that do not. Make sure that the brand you drink doesn't contain gluten. I want you to enjoy your drink, but I also want you to enjoy how your stomach feels the next day.

Ok, let's face it, most people love chocolate and/or candy. Yes, that's right, there is gluten in some candy and chocolate bars. But don't worry, there are a lot of candies that are safe to eat. Make sure you check all the candies before you eat them.

RECIPES

All recipes can use the same amount of regular flour instead of gluten free flour unless noted. All recipes can use the same amount of regular milk instead of almond milk unless noted.

BREAKFAST

Crepes

My cousin owned a sugar shack and we visited her during maple syrup making season. She made these delicious crepes. She had gotten this recipe because she had taken cooking lessons in France.

- 1/4 C sugar
- 1/2 tsp salt
- 1 1/3 C milk (optional— original unsweetened Almond milk)
- 2 egg
- 1 tsp vanilla
- 2 tbsp butter, melted

ROOT INGREDIENTS

- 1/4 C All purpose gluten free flour, ¼ C tapioca flour
- ½ C regular flour

If only making regular crepes, use 1 Cup regular flour

Combine first 6 ingredients and mix for 2 minutes on medium speed. Separate the main ingredients in half to 2 bowls. Add the root ingredients to each bowl and mix well. In a pan or on a griddle, melt 1/4 tsp butter, add the crepe mixture and cook until golden. Always cook the gluten free ones first.

FRUIT TOPPING

In a small pot, add 2 cups of fruit (I used strawberries), 1/3 Cup sugar and 1/3 Cup water. Bring to a boil, cover and reduce to medium heat.

Cook for 5 min. In a separate bowl add 1 tbsp corn starch and 2 tbsp water and mix. Add to boiling fruit and mix in. Continue to cook another 2 min.

Roll up the crepes and add the fruit.

Pumpkin Muffins

BOWL 1

- 2 tsp pumpkin spice
- 1 tsp cinnamon
- 1/2 tsp baking soda
- ½ tsp baking powder

BOWL 2

- 1/3 C vegetable oil
- 1 egg
- 1 ¼ C sugar
- 1 C pumpkin puree

BOWL 3

- 2 tsp baking powder
- ¼ C water

ROOT INGREDIENTS

- ½ C + 1 tbsp rice flour
- ½ C + 1 tbsp regular flour

*If only making regular muffins, use 1-1/4 Cup regular flour

Mix all ingredients of bowl 1 together, bowl 2 together and bowl 3 together. Pour bowl 3 into bowl 1, then pour bowl 1 into bowl 2. Don't overmix. Separate the main ingredients in half to 2 bowls. Add the root ingredients to each bowl and mix well. Add either 1/2 C chocolate chips OR 1/2 C Raisins. Bake at 350 for 15 minutes.

Blueberry Muffins

- 1 C Sugar + 2 tbsp for the top
- ½ C butter, melted
- 2 eggs
- ½ C almond milk
- 1 tsp vanilla
- ½ tsp salt
- 2 tsp baking powder
- 2 1/2 C blueberries (fresh or frozen)

ROOT INGREDIENTS
- ¾ C gluten free All purpose flour
- 1 ½ C regular Flour

*If only making regular muffins, use 2 Cups regular flour

In a large bowl add butter, 1 C sugar, eggs and almond milk, vanilla, salt and mix together. Mix in baking powder. Separate mixture-take 1 Cup mixture put it in a separate bowl (this will be your gluten free muffins). Add ¾ C gluten free All purpose flour and stir. Stir in 1 C Blueberries to mixture. Put in muffin cups. In the first bowl add 1 ½ C regular Flour and stir. Stir in 1 ½ C blueberries to mixture. Put in separate muffin pan. Sprinkle tops with pinch of sugar. Bake 20 minutes at 375.

Makes 10 regular muffins and 4 gluten free.

Zucchini Bread

Do you have a garden? If you do and you get a lot of Zucchini, make this bread, it's delicious!

- 2 C Sugar
- 2 eggs
- ¾ C vegetable oil
- 3 tsp vanilla
- 3 C shredded zucchini
- I tsp salt
- I tsp baking soda
- I tsp baking powder
- 2 ½ tsp cinnamon (optional)
- ½ C raisins (optional)

ROOT INGREDIENTS

- I ½ C gluten free All purpose flour
- I ½ C regular All purpose flour

If only making regular bread, use 3 Cups regular flour

Mix sugar, eggs, oil, vanilla, zucchini, salt, baking soda, baking powder and cinnamon. Take 1 ½ C of mixture and move to a different bowl. To the new bowl add 1 ½ C gluten free All purpose flour and ½ C raisins. Mix well and add mixture to greased bread pan. In the original bowl add 1 ½ C Regular All purpose flour and ½ C raisins. Mix well and add mixture to greased bread pan. Bake at 350 for 40-50 minutes.

Bacon and Egg Omelette

- 1 lb bacon
- 7 eggs
- 2 tbsp corn starch
- 1 tsp salt
- 1 tsp pepper
- 2 C milk (I used unsweetened Almond milk)

Cut the bacon strips into 2 inch sections and cook in a pan for 8 minutes. Meanwhile crack 7 eggs in a bowl and add milk, corn starch, salt and pepper. Using a mixer, mix for 2 minutes. When bacon is more than ¾ cooked add to the egg mixture along with 1 tbsp bacon grease. Mix with a spoon and pour into 11x9 casserole dish. Bake at 450 for 30. Let sit 15 minutes.

Cinnamon French Toast

My dad gave me this recipe after I got married. He said my memere(his mom) would make this when he was young in the 1930's.

- I egg
- I ½ C of milk (I used unsweetened original Almond milk)
- 1/3 C of sugar
- I tbsp cinnamon (optional)
- Gluten free bread slices or regular bread

In a bowl add egg, milk and sugar. Mix ingredients on high speed for 1 minute. Add cinnamon and mix in with a spoon. Melt 1 tsp butter in a pan. Dunk your bread slices in the liquid and cook in a pan on medium heat. The bread will dry out and get a nice brown color. Dunk the gluten free bread first then use the liquid for the regular bread.

Chocolate Zucchini Bread

- 2 C Sugar
- 2 eggs
- ¾ C vegetable oil
- 3 tsp vanilla
- 3 C shredded zucchini
- I tsp salt
- I tsp baking soda
- I tsp baking powder
- ½ C gluten free cocoa powder
- ½ C semisweet chocolate chips

ROOT INGREDIENTS

- I ½ C gluten free All purpose flour
- I ½ C regular All purpose flour

If only making regular bread, use 3 Cups regular flour

Mix sugar, eggs, oil, vanilla, zucchini, salt, baking soda, baking powder and cocoa powder. Take 1 ½ C of mixture and move to a different bowl. To the new bowl add 1 ½ C gluten free All purpose flour and ½ C semisweet chocolate chips. Mix well and add mixture to greased bread pan. In the original bowl add 1 ½ C Regular All purpose flour and ½ C raisins. Mix well and add mixture to greased bread pan. Bake at 350 for 40-50 minutes.

Applesauce

I never saw store bought applesauce in my house growing up. My mom always made her applesauce. So when I got married and had children, they never got store bought either.

Wash 15-18 apples(depending on size)-I use Mcintosh. Cut the apples 2 times(4 pcs) and put in a pot(with skin and seeds). Add water-1/2 of the amount of apples. Bring to a boil, then reduce to medium heat. Cook for 30 minutes-mixing occasionally. Remove from heat and let sit for 30 minutes. Using a metal/mesh strainer, spoon in cooked apples and juice. Push through strainer. Once all the sauce has been strained, discard the skin and seeds. Add 1/2 Cup Sugar while still warm.

Home Fries

- 6 big potatoes, cubed
- I tbsp garlic powder
- I tbsp parsley
- I tbsp paprika
- I tsp salt
- I tsp pepper
- 3 tbsp olive oil

Wash the potatoes and cut them small. Put the potatoes in a bowl and add 1 tbsp olive oil and mix the potatoes with the oil. In a pan heat up 2 tbsp olive and add the cubed potatoes. Add all the ingredients and mix the potatoes around. Cook on medium for 20 minutes, mixing frequently.

Cinnamon Sugar Mini Donuts

- ¾ C gluten free All purpose flour
- ¼ C Tapioca flour
- ½ C sugar
- 1/2 stick butter melted
- 1 tsp baking powder
- ½ C milk (I used unsweetened original
- Almond milk)
- 1 tsp vanilla
- 1 egg(optional)
- ¾ tsp nutmeg

Mix all the ingredients together. I used a mini cake pop maker. Filled the holes 3/4 tsp, baked for 4 minutes. Remove from pan, fill again. While next batch is cooking, roll the donuts in the sugar coating. Repeat process.

SUGAR COATING

- 3/4 tsp cinnamon
- 1/3 Cup sugar

LUNCH

SOUPS, SALADS AND STUFF

Summer Salad

When the weather is hot, who wants to cook and warm up the house? This corn salad can be eaten as a meal or as a side.

- 1 can of corn, water drained
- 1 can black beans, drained
- 1 onion chopped (any kind)
- 1 big tomato or 20 cherry tomatoes cut
- chopped parsely (can use cilantro instead)
- salt and pepper to taste
- 1 tsp minced garlic
- ½ tsp sugar
- squeeze 1-2 limes (to taste)

In a large bowl, mix all the ingredients together. Regrigerate for 2 hours before serving.

Taco Salad

When you are invited to a party, bring something you can eat....it might be the only thing there gluten free. I brought this taco salad and everyone loved it.

- 1 lb hamburger
- 1 pkg gluten free taco seasoning
- 8 oz shredded cheese (I used mexican 4 cheese)
- ½ bag tortilla gluten free chips smashed up
- 1 big bag salad (chopped)
- 1 can sliced olives
- ¾ bottle gluten free catalina dressing
- optional-1 tomato, 1 onion-chopped

Mix everything except hamburger. Cook hamburger, add gluten free taco seasoning, wait for all the water to cook out and add to the salad. Mix everything together.

Grilled Chicken Veggie Quesadillas

No matter what season it is, it's always a good time to cook on the grill. You can also cook these in a pan if the weather is bad. Either way, they taste delicious! This is a good way to sneak in the vegetables to your family for healthy eating.

In a pan marinate vegetables you like with 1 tbsp olive oil for 5 minutes. I used onions, peppers, zucchini, spinach, mushrooms-all cut small. For the chicken, I usually use rotisserie, but any boneless chicken will do. 1 package gluten free wraps. Mexican style shredded cheese. Once the vegetables are done, set them aside. You do the same process for the grill version and the stove. Spray the pan or the wrap with Pam. Put wrap down on pan/grill for 1 min. Flip wrap over, quickly spread out 1 tsp of cheese on half of wrap. Add 1 tbsp veggies. On top of that add few pieces of chicken and then 1 more tsp cheese. Fold wrap over in half. Press down lightly. Flip over one more time for 10 seconds and it is done. It is a quick process of placing the ingredients so the wrap doesn't burn, it would be easier to put all the different ingredients in bowls next to where you are working. Serve it with salsa and sour cream.

Seafood Chowder

In New England we are very fortunate to be able to get fresh seafood. Try this chowder and you will think you are on vacation in New England.

- 3 tbsp butter
- I onion chopped
- I piece salt pork
- 2 cans clams with juice
- 2 stalks celery chopped
- I tsp salt & pepper
- 4 medium potatoes peeled & cut up
- I 46 oz can clam juice
- I tbsp paprika
- I tbsp parsley
- 4 oz gluten free crab meat
- ½ lb scallops
- 4 oz can small shrimps

Melt butter in a big pot. Add salt pork. Let cook for 5 minutes. Add onions and celery and cook for 5 minutes. Add all the other ingredients(including juices from clams). Keep the salt pork in. Bring to a boil, lower to medium heat for 12 minutes. Take the salt pork out. Add........

for white chowder(New england) add 16 oz half/half cream

for the red chowder(Manhattan) add 16 oz can Italian chopped tomatoes

Clam Cakes

Growing up in New England, sum-mertime meant clam cakes and chowder (said like chowda). It took years, but now I get to enjoy the clam cakes again

- ½ C plus 1 tbsp white rice flour
- ¼ C tapioca flour
- ¼ C corn starch
- 1 tbsp baking powder
- 1/2 tsp salt
- 1/2 tbsp sugar
- 1 can clams with juice (6.5 oz)
- 1/8 cup milk (optional-original unsweetened Almond milk)
- vegetable oil

Mix everything together. Cook in hot vegetable oil. Drop 1 tbsp at a time in the oil. Turn them in oil so all the clamcake turns golden brown. Remove clamcake, put on papertowels to aborb oil. Let cool 5 min. Makes a dozen.

Veggie Frittata

I tried a frittata once and it was delish! But now that I have gluten and dairy issues, I thought you had to use cheese and cows milk in a frittata. Not the case. I made this one without cheese and milk and it tasted great. You can use any vegetables you like in yours. I will make this more often and mix up different vegetables and I will try adding some small pieces of partly cooked potatoes.

- 8 eggs
- ¼ C onion-chopped
- ¼ C green pepper-chopped
- ½ C mushrooms-chopped
- 2 Cup spinach-chopped
- 1 clove garlic-chopped
- 2 tbsp olive oil
- 1 tsp salt
- 1 tsp gluten free corn starch
- ½ tsp pepper
- ½ tsp parsley
- ¼ C Almond milk
- ½ C Cheddar cheese (optional-I didn't use)

In a cast iron pan add olive oil. Once hot, add onions, green peppers, mushrooms, parsley, spinach and garlic. Cook for 5 minutes. In a bowl add eggs wisk together salt, pepper, corn starch and almond milk. Once vegetables are cooked, add egg mixture and cheese. Bake at 350 for 30 minutes.

Chicken Noodle Soup

Living in New England there is nothing better on a cool Fall day then soup. I made chicken noodle soup. Let this recipe warm you up.

- 4 C gluten free chicken broth—I use Swanson's
- 1 tsp Herb ox chicken granual
- $\frac{1}{2}$ tsp salt and pepper
- 1 celery stalk chopped
- 2 carrots cut up
- 1 onion chopped
- 2 C of water
- 1 C cooked chicken
- 1 can cut up tomatoes or 3 fresh tomatoes cut up
- 1 C gluten free pasta

In a pot add all the ingredients except the pasta. Bring to a boil, cook for 15 minutes. In a separate pot cook the pasta al dente. Drain water and add to soup for the last 5 minutes of cooking.

Chili

This recipe is 30 years old and everyone loves it.

- 1 lb lean ground beef
- 16 oz canned kidney beans
- 28 oz crushed tomatoes
- 1 C chopped onion
- 1 C chopped celery
- 1 tsp salt & pepper
- 4 tsp chili powder
- ½ tsp garlic powder

Brown the meat in a large pot. Stir in all ingredients. Bring to a boil, lower heat, cover. Cook for 20 minutes stirring occasionally. Let sit for 5 minutes cover off. Can eat with shredded cheese and gluten free tortilla chips.

Kale Soup

This is another Portuguese recipe that my family loves.

- 32 oz gluten free chicken broth
- 4 medium potatoes cut up small
- 2 medium onions chopped
- 6 cloves garlic minced
- 2 bay leaves
- 5 oz Kale chopped
- 1 16 oz can diced tomato
- Salt and pepper to taste
- 1 16 oz can kidney beans
- 1 lb chirico cut small
- 2 tbsp olive oil

In a large pot heat up 2 tbsp olive oil. Add onions and garlic for 5 minutes. Add chirico stir for 3 minutes. Add remaining ingredients. Bring to a boil, reduce heat and cook for 30 minutes.

Venus de Milo Soup

- 1 lb hamburger, fried
- 46 oz gluten free chicken broth
- 32 oz water
- 1 package gluten free onion soup
- 2 celery stalks, cut in small pieces
- Boil above ingredients for 20 minutes

Now add:

- 1 14 oz can cut tomatoes
- 1 package frozen vegetable mix-green beans, carrots, corn
- ½ C small gluten free pasta

Boil for 15 minutes, turn off burner and let sit for 10 minutes

Pasta Fagioli

This recipe came from one of the first cook books I got in 1989. I can't even tell you which book it was, but I have changed the recipe since I first made it. It's hearty, healthy and tasty.

- 1 lb hamburger
- 1 large onion chopped
- 1 large carrot chopped
- 2 large celery stalks chopped
- 2 16 oz cans crushed tomatoes
- 1 tsp basil
- 1 tsp oregano
- 1 tsp parsely
- 1 tsp garlic powder
- ¼ tsp black pepper
- ½ tsp salt
- 3 C gluten free beef broth
- 1 can kidney or black beans(rinsed)
- 8 oz gluten free elbow macaroni

Boil gluten free macaroni separately for 5-6 min, drain.

In a pot, brown meat and crumble until it is brown. Add onion, carrot, celery, tomatoes, seasonings and broth to pot. Cook on med for 15 min, stirring occasionally. Turn off heat. Add macaroni and beans to pot.

Cobb Salad

The first time I made this I was nervous, but now it is so much fun to make for gatherings, parties and holidays. Use the vegetables you like. It differs every time I make it.

- Lettuce
- Spinach
- Carrots-shredded
- Peppers-sliced
- Cherry tomatoes
- Cucumbers-cut up
- Navy beans-rinsed
- Hard boiled eggs-cut in half
- Purple onions-chopped
- Celery-cut up
- Black olives

Place lettuce and spinach on the bottom of dish. Line up the vegetables to make it colorful. Eat with gluten free dressing.

Chicken Pot Pie

- 2 C gluten free chicken broth
- 1 ½ C cooked chicken cut up
- ½ Can peas and carrot mix
- 2 medium potatoes, cubed
- 3 tbsp corn starch
- 1 tsp parsley
- 1 tbsp salt
- 1 tsp pepper
- 1 tsp gluten free granulated bouillon
- Crust-use the crust recipe on page 64

In a pot add chicken broth and bring to a boil. In a separate pot, cook the potatoes. Bring to a boil and let cook for 5 minutes, remove and drain water out. In a bowl mix 3 tbsp corn starch with 4 tbsp water. When broth boiling, add slowly and stir to thicken the broth. Once thickened, add chicken, potatoes, peas and carrots, parsley, salt, pepper and granulated bouillon. Press your crust dough in the bottom of the pie plate(I make it thin). Stir all together and add to your pie plates. Cover with a thin rolled out layer of dough. Press down around the edges with a fork. Put 3 small holes in the top of the dough. Spread thin layer of milk on top of crust to give it a golden brown color. Bake at 375 for 22 minutes.

White Chicken Chili

- 1 C cooked chicken(1 used Rotisserie)
- 1 medium onion chopped
- 1 tbsp olive oil
- 2 cloves of garlic chopped
- 32 oz gluten free chicken broth
- 2 cans small white beans(can use white kidney beans)
- 1 small can chopped green chilies
- 1 ½ tsp cumin
- 2 tsp oregano
- ½ tsp cayenne pepper
- 1 tsp parsley
- salt/pepper to taste
- optional: chopped jalepeno

Marinate onions and garlic in olive oil-5 min. Add broth, chilies, cumin, oregano, cayenne powder, salt, pepper and parsley and bring to a boil. Add beans and reduce heat, cook 15 min. Add chicken and cook additional 10 minutes.

Potato Salad

We have tried many different potato salads, but my sister's recipe is the best.

- 6 large potatoes cut up
- 6 eggs boiled, peeled and cut into pieces
- 3 tbsp mayonaise
- I celery stalk cut into tiny pieces
- I tsp salt, pepper, onion powder
- paprika

Boil the cut up potatoes for 10 minutes, drain and transfer to a bowl to cool. Once potatoes are cooled add cut up boiled eggs, mayonaise, celery, salt, pepper, onion powder and mix all together. Once all mixed sprinkle paprika on top. Let cool in refrigerator for few hours.

DINNER

Baked Stuffed Zucchini

- 2 medium zucchinis
- ½ C ricotta cheese
- ¾ C mozzarella cheese
- I C sauce-I used Ragu traditional
- ½ lb hamburger
- ½ tsp each of basil, oregano, parsley, garlic powder, salt, pepper
- I egg

FILLING

Cook hamburger and add all the spices and 1 egg. Once done, put in a bowl and add 1/4 cup mozzarella cheese, ricotta cheese, 3/4 cup sauce and mix them together.

Using a potato peeler, peel 1st slice off zucchini and throw away. Continue to peel slices off zucchini(s). Make an X with 4 slices and put in a big tablespoon of the filling. Fold over the 4 sections of zucchini slices to cover. Makes 8-10

Use a 13x9 cassarole dish. Coat the bottom with a thin layer of sauce. Add the stuffed zucchinis. Add a little sauce over each one. Add the balance of mozzarella cheese over the sauce. Bake at 400 for 20 minutes, or until cheese is completely melted.

Maifun

- ½ C onions, cut
- ½ C peppers, cut
- ½ C mushrooms, cut
- ½ C celery, cut
- 1 tbsp olive oil
- 20 shrimps
- ½ tsp parsley
- ½ tsp garlic powder
- Salt/pepper to tase
- 1 lemon
- 32 oz gluten free chicken broth
- 4 oz maifun rice sticks
- 1-14 oz can chopped tomatoes

In a pan, use 1tbsp of olive oil, add vegetables for 5 minutes on med heat then add shrimps (I used frozen, already cooked). Add parsely, garlic powder and salt/pepper to taste. Squeeze juice of 1 lemon.

While that is cooking, in a pot add 32 oz gluten free chicken broth and bring to boil. Add Maifun rice sticks, reduce heat to low and cook for 2 minute(they cook fast). Once noodles are cooked add noodles and remaining broth to shrimps and vegetables. Add tomatoes. Let cook on med heat until most of broth is gone. Let sit 5 minutes.

Fish

- 1lb Cod or Haddock
- 1 C gluten free plain bread crumbs
- ½ C Rice flour
- ½ C gluten free All purpose flour
- 1 hot sauce
- 1 pkg con azafran
- ½ tsp salt
- Olive oil

Put all dry ingredients in a shallow bowl or a plate. Heat olive oil in a pan. Cut up the fish to individual portions. Hit each piece of fish with 1 small splash of hot sauce and roll in the mixture till completely coated. Put in the pan. Cook for 5 min, then flip over. Do the same to remaining fish. Fish will be crispy.

Chips—Healthy French Fries

Most restaurants and fast food places do not offer gluten free french fries. The oil is used for other fried foods so it is not safe to eat it. My stomach cannot handle fried foods. These baked french fries are delicious!

It doesn't matter what type of potato you use. I always wash them and leave the skin on. Cut up 6 medium potatoes and put in a bowl. Add 3 tablespoons of olive oil and sea salt. Mix all together. Preheat oven to 450 degrees. Put the french fries on sprayed cookie sheets in the oven for 30 minutes. Flip them half way through cooking.

Meatloaf

- 1lb lean hamburger
- 1 onion-shredded
- ½ tsp garlic powder, basil, oregano, parsley, salt and pepper
- 2 eggs
- ¾ C plain gluten free bread crumbs
- 1 tbsp ketchup

Mix all the ingredients in a bowl. Spray an 9x9 casserole with non stick spray. Spread out the meatloaf and cook at 400 for 30 minutes. Drain any meat fat out of casserole before serving.

Jambalaya

I got this recipe back in the early 1990's. Over the years I've changed the recipe but this is our favorite. The great thing about Jambalaya is that you change up the protein you put in it. I always put 2 proteins, usually 2 of these: chicken, chorizo, shrimps, polish sausage, hamburger. Any 2 of these will give you a great meal.

- 2 celery stalks chopped
- I medium onion chopped
- ½ green sweet pepper chopped
- I-14 oz can cut tomatoes
- 2 tbsp butter
- 2 C gluten free chicken broth
- 2/3 C white rice
- I tsp basil
- 1/2 tsp garlic powder
- 1/2 tsp pepper
- 1/2 tps hot pepper sauce
- I bay leaf
- 2 C of protein (mentioned above-I cup of each)

In a large pan, cook the 2 cups of protein in 1tbsp olive oil for 3 minutes. Remove, set aside. In the large pan add 2tbsp butter, melt then add celery, onion and sweet pepper until tender. Add all the ingredients. I add the rice last. Mix everything up. Bring to a boil, lower heat to simmer and cover for 20 minutes

Stuffed Cabbage (Golumpki)

- 32 oz gluten free chicken broth
- 2 ½ lbs hamburger
- 1 ½ C rice
- 2 medium onions, chopped
- 1 large head of cabbage (de-cored)

Bring a large pot of water to a boil, add head of cabbage for 25 minutes. After 15 minutes of boiling, try separating leaves off head with tongs. Once done, drain water and add cabbage leaves to cold water. Let them sit there for 30 minutes. Take 1 leaf at a time and add 1 tbsp worth of raw hamburger, 1 tbsp onions, 1 tbsp rice and a pinch of salt. Fold in the sides of leaf and roll the ingredients up. Put in a large pot. Add the chicken broth to cover. Cover the pot and bake at 400 for 1 1/2 hours. Take out of the oven and let sit for 30 minutes with the cover on.

BBQ Ribs

This is the easiest recipe with the best tasting Ribs

- 6 lbs Pork ribs
- Water
- I bottle gluten free BBQ sauce

Place ribs facing meat down in a big cassarole pan on the stove-I cover 2 burners. Fill 1/4 of the pan with water. Bring to a boil. Cover pan, reduce to simmer for 2 hours. Drain out the water. I cut them down to sets of 3 ribs, put back in the pan. Cover with barbecue Sauce

Pizza

- 1 ¼ C gluten free All purpose flour
- ½ tsp baking powder
- ½ tsp salt
- ½ tsp xanthan gum
- ¾ tsp instant yeast
- ½ tbsp. honey
- ½ C warm water
- 1 tbsp olive oil
- 1 tsp buttermilk powder (1 used 1 tsp coffee mate)
- 3 tbsp tomato sauce
- ¼ C mozzarella cheese
- pepperoni

In first bowl mix the dry ingredients together. In a smaller bowl add honey, warm water, olive oil, yeast and ½ C of dry mixture. Stir to combine, lumps are ok. Set aside for 20 minutes, until the mixture is bubbly and smells yeasty. Add wet mixture to dry ingredients along with the coffee mate and knead dough until dough not sticky anymore (add a little flour if sticky). Put dough on pizza pan and press it out to 9 inch round with ¼-1/2 thick. Spread 3 tbsp sauce on dough. Add mozzarella and pepperoni. Bake at 425 for 20 minutes, until cheese if fully melted. Let sit 15 minutes.

This was based on a recipe I found at www.kingarthurflour.com

Hamburger Delight

Growing up the youngest of 4, my parents had a tight budget. I always liked this dish and so did my kids.

- 1 lb hamburger
- 1 package birds eye mixed vegetables
- Uncle Ben original rice

RICE

Boil 2 1/2 cups water, 1 cup rice, 2 tbsp olive oil and 2 full cloves of garlic de-skinned for 15 min.

HAMBURGER

Cook on stove, mash up until no pink-add 1/2 tsp salt and pepper and 1 tsp onion powder.

BIRDS EYE VEGETABLE

cook in microwave for 4 minutes. Once all are done, combine in a bowl.

Balsamic Chicken

- ½ C gluten free chicken broth
- ½ C balsamic vinegar
- 2 tsp honey
- 1 tbsp butter
- 1 tbsp olive oil
- 5 boneless chicken breasts
- ¼ tsp salt
- ¼ tsp pepper
- ½ C gluten free All purpose flour
- 1 small shallot, chopped
- 1 tsp parsley

In a bowl, combine first 3 ingredients, set aside. Add salt and pepper to chicken then dredge the chicken in the flour. In a pan melt butter and add oil. Add chicken to pan, cook for 3 minutes on each side or until golden brown. Once done, put chicken aside. In the same pan add the shallots and saute for 30 seconds. Add the broth mixture. Bring to a boil for 3 minutes. Pour over the cooked chicken.

Chicken Stew

It took me years to get this stew yummy

- 1 ½ C cooked chicken cubed(I use rotisserie)
- 1 carrot-peeled and chopped
- 1 small onion-chopped
- 1 C fresh or frozen beans-chopped
- 2 small potatoes-peeled and cut in cubes
- 32 oz gluten free chicken broth
- ½ tsp gluten free chicken bouillon
- 1 tsp parsley
- ½ tsp salt and pepper
- ½ tsp garlic salt
- 1 can cut tomatoes(optional)
- 1 heaping tbsp gluten free corn starch
- 1/2 C water

Add all ingredients to pot except tomatoes. corn starch and 3/4 Cup water. Bring to a boil, reduce medium heat for 15 minutes. Optional—Add can of cut tomatoes and bring back to a boil. In a bowl mix corn starch and 3/4 Cup water. Once stew is boiling again, slowly add the corn starch/water mixture while mixing the stew with a spoon. Let stew boil 1 minute. Shut stove off and let stew sit for 10 minutes.

Rice Pilaf

- 2 ½ C gluten free chicken broth
- ½ onion-chopped
- 1 carrot-chopped
- 2 tbsp butter
- ¼ tsp parsley
- ¼ tsp pepper
- ½ tsp salt
- 1 C rice

In a pot, melt butter over medium heat. Cook the chopped onion for 2-3 minutes. Stir in 2 tbsp rice and cook for 5 minutes, stirring frequently. Add the remaining ingredients and bring to a boil. Lower the heat and cover the pot. Cook for 18 minutes.

Fried Rice

This is a staple dish my mom makes with a Sunday family meal.

- 1 green bell pepper-chopped
- 1 onion-chopped
- ½ C mushrooms-chopped
- 3 tbsp gluten free soy sauce
- 3 tbsp olive oil
- ½ tsp salt and pepper
- 1 tsp parsley
- 1 tsp garlic powder
- 4 C long grain rice
- 2 C cooked chicken cut up (optional)

The recipe works better if you cook the rice the night before, but if you make the rice on the same day, just let it cool first. In a pan heat 2 tbsp olive oil. Add pepper, onion, mushrooms, salt, pepper, parsley and garlic powder. Cook until tender, approximately 5 min. Mix in chicken, then mix in rice. Stir all the ingredients together. Add 1 tbsp olive oil and 3 tbsp soy sauce, or to taste.

Seafood Pasta with White Sauce

I took ingredients we love and made this tasty dish.

- 10 ounce gluten free pasta
- ½ onion chopped
- 3 garlic cloves chopped
- ½ C white wine
- 1 lemon
- 1 tbsp butter
- 2 tbsp olive oil
- 10-12 shrimps
- 1 6oz can chopped clams
- ½ tsp parsley
- 1/8 tsp crushed red peppers

Heat 2 tbsp olive oil and add onion and garlic-marinate for 1 minute. Add butter. Add shrimps and cook until they turn pink. Add chopped clams with the juice, 1/2 cup white wine, juice from a whole lemon, parsley, crushed red pepper, salt and pepper to taste. Add the pasta and the 1 cup of reserved pasta water. Turn off burner. Mix and let sit for 10 minutes

Cook the pasta separately. Drain the water but reserve 1 Cup.

Sticky Wings

Tasty dish to bring to a party.

- **8 lbs chicken wings**
- 10 ounces gluten free soy sauce
- 2 cups light brown sugar
- 12 ounces gluten free molasses
- garlic powder

Place frozen wings on 2 large cookie sheets and liberally douse them with garlic powder. Cook them in the oven at 350 for 45 minutes turning the wings every 20 minutes and draining the liquid.

Using a deep pot, add soy sauce, molasses and brown sugar and bring to a boil. Boil to reduce liquid for 15 minutes stirring often. Add wings to a baking dish and cover with the reduced liquid. Cook in the oven for 45-60 minutes, basting every 15 minutes.

Baked Stuffed Shrimps

My mother in law is Portuguese and she would make us these stuffed shrimps on the fourth of July. Eventually that stopped but my family loved them. So I took an old recipe and made it gluten free.

- 25 Jumbo cooked shrimps-butterflied
- 3/4 stick of butter
- 2 onions-chopped
- 4 pcs garlic-chopped
- 1 tsp parsley
- 1 tsp paprika
- 2 eggs-beaten in separate bowl
- 1/2 tsp salt and pepper

- 7 hits of hot sauce
- 1/2 lb scallops-chopped
- 1/2 lb shrimps-chopped
- 12 ounce gluten free bread-put under water, squeeze out water and break into pieces

Butterfly the shrimps but keep the tails on. Put shrimps on a sprayed cookie sheet-do not use foil.

In a pan melt butter add onion, garlic and paprika-5 minutes. Add chopped scallops and shrimps and stir for 10 minutes. Add pieces of bread, hot sauce, salt and pepper-cook on low for 10 min-Keep stirring to Mix and break up the bread. When done turn off burner but keep mixing to cool off the stuffing for 5 minutes. Add the 2 beaten eggs and stir the stuffing mixture.

Use a large tablespoon to scoop stuffing on the shrimp. Bake at 350 for 25 minutes

Pasta Sauce

- 1 28 oz can San Marzano peeled tomatoes
- 2 24.5 oz Italian tomato puree
- 1 5 oz Italian tomato paste
- 2 tbsp olive oil
- 2 tbsp butter
- 4 cloves of garlic-minced
- 1 tbsp fresh or dried basil
- Salt and pepper to taste
- 1 tbsp fresh or dried parsley
- 1 lb hamburger
- 2 C gluten free chicken broth

Add olive oil to pan, cook garlic for 1 minute, add hamburger and mash up. Once hamburger is cooked, add all the other ingredients. Bring sauce to boil, reduce heat to low and cook for 30 minutes.

PASTA

In a separate pot, bring water to a boil, add 1 tbsp salt and the gluten free pasta. Reduce heat and cook approximately 10 minutes. Once pasta is done, reserve 2 cups of pasta water and add to sauce-It thickens the sauce.

Chickpea Noodle Casserole

- 1 tbsp olive oil
- ½ C baby bella mushrooms
- ½ onion chopped fine
- ½ small jalapeno diced
- 2 cloves garlic minced
- 1 ¼ tsp almond butter
- 1 tbsp gluten free All purpose flour
- 1 C water
- 1 C unsweetened almond milk
- 4 ounces gluten free pasta
- ½ C frozen peas-thawed
- 1/2(8 oz) can Chickpeas-drained
- 1 ½ tbsp plain Kale chips (mashed up)
- Sea salt and pepper to taste

In a large pan, heat olive oil on medium heat and add mushrooms. Add salt and pepper, cook 3 min. Add onions, jalapeno, garlic and a little more salt. Cook for 10 min, stirring occasionally. Add flour over vegetables and stir to combine. Add water and lightly scrape the bottom of the pan to deglaze, then stir in the almond milk. Let it reduce for 20 minutes over medium heat until thickened. Add the mashed up kale chips and a little more salt and pepper.

In a medium pot, bring water to a boil and cook 4 oz of gluten free pasta and add salt. Cook 4 minutes less than package says. Once done, save 1/2 cup pasta water, drain the rest.
In a separate bowl, mash the 4 oz chickpeas.

Add the reserved pasta water, chickpeas and green peas to the mushroom sauce and stir to combine. Lastly, add the gluten free pasta and stir it all together letting it continue to cook for 5 minutes. You can also add grilled/rotisserie chicken to this.

This was based on a recipe from The Chew

Honey Barbeque Chicken Wings

- **5 lbs chicken wings**
- **3 tsp garlic powder**
- **¼ C olive oil**
- **2 tsp paprika**
- **1 tsp salt**
- **½ tsp pepper**
- **6 tbsp butter**
- **2 C barbeque sauce**
- **½ C honey**
- **6 hits of hot sauce**

Put the chicken wings in a big bowl, add garlic powder, olive oil, paprika, salt and pepper. Mix it all up. Put on cooling rack on cookie sheet. Bake at 400 for 45 minutes.

While wings are cooking make the sauce. In a pot add barbeque sauce, honey, hot sauce and butter. Bring to a boil, lower to simmer for 5 minutes. Once Chicken wings are done, put in big bowl and add sauce and mix. Put chicken wings back on the cooling racks on the cookie sheet and broil on low for 5 minutes

DESSERT

Flourless Chocolate Cake

- 1 C semi sweet chocolate chips
- 8 tbsp (1 stick) salted butter
- ¾ C sugar
- ¼ tsp salt
- 1 tsp vanilla
- 3 eggs
- ½ C unsweetend cocoa powder

Preheat oven to 375. Grease 8 inch round cake pan. Cut wax paper to fit bottom and grease it too.

CAKE:

Put chocolate chips and butter in microwave and heat until the butter is melted and chocolate is soft. Stir together until all is melted. Stir in sugar, salt and vanilla. In a separate bowl wisk the eggs then add to mixture as well as the cocoa. Mix everything just to combine. Pour into cake pan. Bake 25 min. Remove from oven, let sit for 5 minutes. Loosen edges with a knife and turn over on a serving plate. Has to cool completely before glazing (30 min to 1 hr).

GLAZE

- 1 C semi sweet chocolate chips
- 1/2 C heavy cream

Combine chocolate chips and cream in a bowl. Put in microwave and heat for 1-2 minutes, stir until chocolate melts. Might need another minute in microwave.

Once melted, pour over the cake.

This was based on a recipe I found at www.kingarthurflour.com

Peanut Butter Cookies

- 1 C sugar
- 1 C peanut butter
- 1 tsp baking soda
- 1 egg

Mix all the ingredients to-gether. Roll into balls, put on cookie sheet. Press down with fork, sprinkle with sugar. Bake at 350 for 8 min, move to cooling rack.

Apple Pie

Fall is apple picking time. I go out with my family and we pick lots of apples. They always expect a tasty apple pie as their reward.

- **8 big apples (macintosh) peeled and cut up**
- **½ C sugar**
- **½ tsp nutmeg and all spice**
- **1 tsp cinnamon**
- **1 tbsp corn starch**
- **4 tbsp butter (cut up)**

Crust-recipe on page 64

In a large bowl add apples, sugar, nutmeg, all spice, cinnamon and cornstarch and mix all together. Transfer apples to crust. Add the pieces of butter over the apples. Put the other crust on top and pinch the bottom and top crust together at the edges. Brush the crust with milk/almond milk and Bake at 350 for 50-60 minutes.

Pastry Crust

My mom has always insisted on making homemade pies for the holidays-including the crust. I had to change it when I became gluten free, but I have added the original and the gluten free one for your family. They both make a 9 inch pie or 3 mini's.

GLUTEN FREE CRUST

- 1 ½ C gluten free All purpose flour
- ½ C tapioca flour
- ¼ tsp salt
- ½ C shortening
- 1 egg
- ½ tsp vinegar
- 1 tsp xanthan gum

Put all the ingredients in a bowl and kneed the ingredients together until dough is not sticky. Can use right away.

ORIGINAL CRUST

- 2 C flour
- ½ tsp salt
- 2/3 C shortening
- 2 tbsp cold water
- 1 egg
- ½ vinegar

Put all the ingredients in a bowl and kneed the ingredients together until dough is not sticky. Can use right away.

Strawberry Banana Oat Bars

- 2 cups gluten free rolled oats
- ¾ C Strawberry preserves
- 1 tsp baking powder
- 2 bananas smashed
- ¼ C maple syrup
- 1 tsp vanilla extract

Place 1 cup oatmeal in food processor or blender and pulse until you get a flour. Pour the flour and regular oatmeal into a bowl and stir in baking powder. Add mashed bananas, vanilla and maple syrup. Stir to combine. Separate mixture in half. Place one half of mixture in a foil lined 8x8 dish. Spread preserves on top. Sprinkle the other half of oat mixture over the top. Bake at 375 degrees for 35 minutes.

Graham Cracker Pie

I grew up in a Canadian family and the Holiday's always included this pie.

CRUST—*ROOT INGREDIENTS*

- 7.5 oz gluten free graham crackers or 1 package regular graham crackers
- 4 tbsp butter-melted
- ¼ C sugar
- Mix all together and push down evenly in a pie plate (leave 1 tbsp for later) Bake in oven 400 for 7 minutes

FILLING

- 17 oz unsweetened original Almond milk (can use regular milk)
- 5 tbsp sugar
- 2 ½ tsp corn starch
- 4 egg yolks (keep egg whites for meringue-put in fridge for 10 min)

In a large pot add 4 yolks, almond milk, sugar, corn starch and vanilla and cook on high heat. Continuously stirring until it boils and thickens-approximately 4 minutes. Add to the baked crust.

MERINGUE

- 4 egg whites, chilled
- 8 tbsp sugar
- ½ tsp cream of tartar

Add 4 chilled egg whites and cream of tartar to a bowl. Use mixer on high for 1 minute. Add sugar, continue with mixer for 45 seconds. Plop on top of filling around pie plate and use a fork to make sure all is covered. Add remaining 1 tbsp graham crackers on top of meringue. Bake at 400 approximately for 10 minutes-until golden brown. Cool on shelf for 3 hours, then chill in fridge 2 hours before serving.

Chocolate Coconut Cookie

- 1-14 oz bag sweetened coconut flakes
- 2 C Semi-sweet chocolate chips
- 2/3 C chopped lightly salted almonds
- 1-14 oz can sweetened condensed milk
- 1 egg (optional)

In a bowl combine coconut, chocolate chips, egg, almonds and sweetened condensed milk, stir until combined.

Scoop out teaspoon size onto cookie sheet. Moisten fingers with water and shape into ovals and pat tops flat. Bake cookies for 12 to 14 minutes. Cool on baking sheet.

Bean Pie

My husband and I frequent a local traditional Portuguese restaurant that offers this pie. We get it every time we go if they have it. It sells out quickly so I found this recipe to enjoy any time I want.

- 2-15 oz cans navy beans, rinsed and drained
- 1-12 oz can evaporated milk
- ½ C butter, melted
- 1 teaspoon cinnamon
- 1 teaspoon nutmeg
- 2 tablespoons gluten free All purpose flour
- 2 C sugar
- 2 tablespoons vanilla extract
- 2 eggs
- 2 egg yolks

In a blender, place the navy beans, evaporated milk, melted butter, cinnamon, nutmeg, flour, sugar, vanilla extract, eggs, and egg yolks and blend until smooth—about 1 minute. Pour the filling into the pie plate. Bake at 450 degrees for 15 minutes, then reduce heat to 350 degrees and bake an additional 35 minutes until the filling is set and the crust is golden brown. Cool for 1 hour, cover top with powdered sugar. Keep in Refrigerator

Date Squares

My mom has been making these for years but I haven't been able to have them until I changed the recipe to gluten free. They are delish!

DATE FILLING:

- 3 C pitted dates chopped
- I ½ C water
- I C light brown sugar

CRUMBLE:

- I C packed light brown sugar
- I C butter, softened (margarine optional)
- ½ tsp salt
- ½ tsp baking soda
- I ½ C gluten free Quick cooking oats

ROOT INGREDIENTS

- ¾ C +I tbsp gluten free All purpose flour
- ¾ C +I tbsp regular All purpose flour

*If only making regular date squares, use 1-3/4 Cup regular flour

DATE FILLING:

Place all ingredients into a large pot and bring to a boil. Reduce heat to low and stir often until consistency is thicker.

DIRECTIONS:

Prepare date filling. Preheat oven to 400. Spray or grease 2 9x8 pans.

Mix together softened butter and brown sugar. Add remaining ingredients except flours. Separate mixture in half put in separate bowls and add gluten free flour to one and regular flour to the other. Press half of the gluten free mixture to the pan and spread half of the date filling. Add remaining gluten free on top of date filling. Does not have to cover completely. Do the same with the Regular flour mixture/filling. Bake for 25 minutes or until golden brown. Let cool 30 minutes.

Raspberry Crumble

A friend of mine gave me this recipe that had gluten in it so I changed it so I could enjoy it.

- 6 tbsp butter
- 6 tbsp light brown sugar
- 1 1/8 C gluten free all-purpose flour or same portion with regular flour
- ½ C gluten free rolled oats
- 1-21oz can of gluten free Raspberry pie filling

In a pan, melt butter. Remove from burner, add brown sugar and mix. Add flour and oats. Spray 9x9 casserole dish with Pam. "Drop" 3/4 mixture with a spoon at bottom of pan. Add raspberry filling. "Drop" remaining mixture on top of raspberry. Bake at 375 for 40 minutes.

Crème Brulee

- 2 C heavy cream
- 2 tsp vanilla
- 4 large egg yolks
- ½ C sugar

In a sauce pan, over medium heat add the cream and vanilla. Bring to a simmer and steep for 1-2 minutes.

In a large bowl add the egg yolks and sugar, whisk until pale and fluffy.

Temper the egg mixture into the hot cream by pouring ¼ C of hot cream into the eggs and whisking to combine. Whisk another ¼ C of hot cream into the eggs. Pour the rest of the hot cream into the egg mixture and whisk. Fill the ramekins ¾ full.

Pour hot water into a 13x9 roasting pan ¼ way up the sides. Put the ramekins into the water of the roasting pan. Water should go up ½ way up the ramekins. Place in a preheated oven of 325 for 30-40 minutes, until the centers are set but slightly jiggly. Remove from the water bath to cool. Refrigerate 2 hours before serving.

TO SERVE:

Gently dab the tops of the custard with a paper towel if there is condensation. Sprinkle top evenly with sugar. Torch to brulee the tops.

This was based on a recipe from The Chew

Chocolate Peanut Butter Balls

- 2 C peanut butter
- ¼ C butter, melted
- 2 C confectioner's sugar
- 3-1 inch pieces of paraffin wax
- 2-11.5 oz bags milk chocolate

ROOT INGREDIENTS

- 1 ½ C rice crisps
- 1 ½ C gluten free rice crisps

If only making regular peanut butter balls, use 3 Cups regular rice crisps

Mix butter and peanut butter together. Add confectioner's sugar and mix. Separate mixture in half. Move half to another bowl. In one bowl add rice crisps. In another bowl add gluten free rice crisps. Roll 1 inch balls and put aside. Use a double burner to melt the chocolate and wax, stirring frequently. Start with the gluten free balls. Place a few in the melted chocolate and roll around until fully covered (I use 2 forks). Move the chocolate balls to a foil topped cookie sheet. Cover all the balls. Cool for ½ hour then put in the refrigerator for 1 hour. Can freeze for 6 months.

Strawberry Rhubarb Treat

What to do in the spring time when the strawberries and rhubarb are coming to life in the garden? I admit it, I've had strawberry rhubarb (pie) years ago, but I've never worked with it. I made this treat and it is a yummy dessert.

- 2-8 inch pieces of rhubarb cut up
- 3 cups strawberries-fresh or frozen
- ¼ C water
- 1/8 C sugar

Add ingredients to pot and bring to a boil. Reduce heat and cook for 10 minutes. After 5 minutes of boiling, Mash fuits in the pot.

In another pot add 1/2 Cup water and bring to a boil. Add 1/2 tsp agar powder, boil for 2 minutes then add this syrup to the fruit. It thickens the fruit when chilled.

Fill 6-4oz containers. Chill for 1 hour.

Coconut Custard Pie

- 3 eggs
- ¾ C sugar
- I C milk (I used unsweetened original Almond milk)
- ¼ C corn starch
- I tsp vanilla
- ¼ C butter, melted
- ½ C flaked sweetened coconut

In a bowl add first 6 ingredients. Mix on medium for 2 minutes. Add coconut and stir in with a spoon. Add mixture to a 9 inch pie plate. Bake on 350 for 45-50 minutes, until top light golden color. Let cool 1 hour, then put in the refrigerator.

Potpouri

Appetizers, party favorites or just a snack

Salsa

Summertime is that time of year when the tomatoes are ready to be picked from the garden. Somehow they all seem to get red at the same time. What to do with them? Salsa!

- 4 large tomatoes
- ½ medium onion
- 2 gloves garlic, minced
- ½ C cilantro or parsely chopped
- I jalapeno pepper seeded and chopped
- juice of I lime
- pinch of sugar
- salt to taste

Cut tomatoes into small pieces. Add the rest of the ingredients. Refrigerate until serving time. Enjoy with gluten free tortillas.

Deviled Eggs

- 1 dozen eggs
- 2 tbsp mayonnaise
- 1 tsp onion powder
- paprika

Put eggs in a pot and cover with water. Boil for 15 minutes. Once they are cooled, peel the shell off. Cut eggs in half. Move the yolk to a bowl. Place the egg halves on a plate. Mash the yolks add 2 tbsp of mayonaise and 1 tsp onion powder and combine. Put 1 tsp yolk mixture in each egg white. Once complete, sprinkle paprika over the eggs.

Bean Dip

- 1 ½ lb hamburger (I use 90%)
- 16 oz salsa
- 16 oz can of refried beans
- Gluten free tortilla chips

In a pan, cook the hamburger completely. Add refried bean, mix them into the meat. Add the salsa and mix completely. That's it, it's done. Enjoy with gluten free tortilla chips.

Stuffed Mushrooms

- 18 regular sized mushrooms (washed and stem/middle removed and chopped)
- ¼ green bell pepper-chopped
- ½ onion-chopped
- 1 tbsp olive oil
- 1 tbsp butter
- 4 large cooked shrimps-chopped or 1/2 can small shrimps
- ½ tsp garlic powder, pepper, parsley
- 1 tsp salt
- ½ C rice
- 1 C gluten free chicken broth
- 2 tbsp gluten free bread crumbs

In a pot, cook the 1/2 Cup of rice (follow directions on package) leave 2 tbsp liquid in rice. In a large pan add olive oil and melt the butter. Add chopped mushroom pieces, bell pepper and onion. Marinate for 3-5 minutes. Add chicken broth, salt, garlic powder, pepper, parsley and shrimps. Stir all together. Add cooked rice (with liquid) and 2 tbsp bread crumbs. Put the mushroom caps in a casserole dish. Scoop a tablespoon worth of stuffing on top of the mushrooms. Bake at 350 for 25 minutes.

DRINKS

A lot of alcohols have gluten in them. I personally like wine,
which is naturally gluten free. Here is a shortcut when making drinks.
An average shot glass is 2 oz or 4 tbsp

Sangria

- 1 Bottle white wine
- 1 lemon cut into wedges
- 1 lime cut into wedges
- 1 orange cut into wedges
- 2 tbsp sugar
- splash of orange juice or lemonade
- 2 shots of vodka
- 1 C raspberries, strawberries or blueberries
- 1 small can diced pineapples
- 4 C ginger ale or sprite

Pour wine into a large pitcher and squeeze the juice wedges from the lemon, lime and orange into the wine. Add pineapple, sugar, orange juice, berries, ginger ale and vodka. If you want to chill overnight, don't add berries nor ginger ale till next day.

Mojito

- Juice of 1 lime
- 2 tsp sugar
- 1 cup ice
- 12 fresh mint leaves
- ¼ C rum
- 4 oz club soda.

Stir together lime juice and sugar until sugar dissolved. Add 2 mint leaves and muddle without breaking them. Add 1 cup ice, rum and club soda. Add 2 more mint leaves and push them through the ice a few times. Take the remaining 8 mint leaves in your hand. Clap your hands together to bruise the leaves to induce the mint juice out. Put the leaves in the glass pushing them through the ice. Garnish with slice of lime.

Strawberry Margarita

- 3 tbsp Tequila
- 1 ½ tbsp. Cointreau triple sec
- ½ lime squeezed
- 8 oz water
- 1 C ice
- 1 tsp sugar
- 4 frozen strawberries (1 for decoration)

Add all the ingredients in a blender on high for 1 minute. If you want to add salt to the rim of the glass, just wet the outer rim and put it in salt. Garnish with a strawberry.

Sea Breeze

- 2 oz grapefruit juice
- 3 oz vodka
- 8 oz cranberry juice
- 1 C ice
- 1 lime wedge

Put all the ingredients juice in a shaker except the lime wedge. Shake to combine. Pour into a glass and garnish with a wedge of lime.

Cosmopolitan

- 1 ½ oz vodka
- ½ oz triple sec
- 4 oz cranberry juice
- Juice of 1 lime

Put all the ingredients in a shaker with ice. Shake to combine then strain into a martini glass. Garnish with a wedge of lime.

Wine

CPSIA information can be obtained
at www.ICGtesting.com
Printed in the USA
BVOW11s0028090218

507645BV00010B/59/P